I Am Gifted Vision Workbook

By Natasha James

Copyright © 2019 by Natasha James

All rights reserved. No part of this publication may be reproduced by any means, graphics, electronic, or mechanical, including photocopying, recording, taping, or by any information storage retrieval system without the written permission of the publisher except in the case of brief quotations embodied in critical articles and reviews.

Natasha James/Rejoice Essential Publishing

PO BOX 512

Effingham, SC 29541

www.republishing.org

Author's website:

Unless otherwise indicated, scripture is taken from the King James Version.

Scripture quotations marked MSG are taken from THE MESSAGE, copyright © 1993, 2002, 2018 by Eugene H. Peterson. Used by permission of NavPress. All rights reserved. Represented by Tyndale House Publishers, Inc.

Scripture quotations marked NASB are taken from the New American Standard Bible® (NASB), Copyright © 1960, 1962, 1963, 1968, 1971, 1972, 1973, 1975, 1977, 1995 by The Lockman Foundation Used by permission. www.Lockman.org"

Scripture quotations marked AMPC are taken from the Amplified® Bible (AMPC), Copyright © 1954, 1958, 1962, 1964, 1965, 1987 by The Lockman Foundation Used by permission. www.Lockman.org"

I Am Gifted Vision Workbook/ Natasha James

ISBN-10: 1-946756-67-9

ISBN-13: 978-1-946756-67-1

A special thank you to my husband for your help and to Tracie McClinton of Very Blessed Events for designing the cover.

The contents of this journal were compiled for an annual women's fellowship I had the honor of hosting, The Gathering of God's Daughter's. The theme of the fellowship in 2019 was "*Purged, Purified and Postured*"! For the past three years, the Gathering of God's Daughter's has met in Durham, North Carolina. Women from across the United States gather together for three days of prayer, praise, and worship, preaching/teaching of the word of God, prophetic declarations, food, and fun! During one of the day sessions, I excitedly presented my guests with this *Gifts and Vision book!* I am super excited to share a space to journal ideas as the LORD gives you instructions. You have a dedicated place to develop these ideas and write your vision. This workbook is a thought-provoking tool used to identify, expand, and help you operate in your spiritual gifts and talents.

You may be asking yourself, "What do the words *Purged, Purified and Postured* have to do with gifts, talents, and vision?" The theme relates to the vision I have been given to bring people into a place of prayer/mediation, where they would begin **purging** of the old spirit man. From the purging, they would begin **purifying** from anything toxic in their life. Once purging and purifying begins, it is my prayer that God would begin to download new revelations and assignments to you. There will even be an awareness of assignments you did not complete due to distractions or discouragements. My prayer is that you will return and or begin to operate in your gifts and callings in order to fulfill the kingdom assignments God has called you to do. I pray that you become '**postured**' – positioned in fixed in, settled in your gifting and able to operate from a divine place of excellence to the glory of God! The theme scripture for this vision is taken from 2 Tim. 1:6, Apostle Paul writes to Timothy to remind him of the gift handed down from the laying of hands, and he encourages him to go forth in ministry. Paul admonishes Timothy to stir up the gift of God that is in him. I Corinthians 12 serves as a back drop to reference spiritual gifts (ministry gifts). However, I also want you to think about gifts and talents as it pertains to your business or how it operates in the marketplace.

As you begin this journey of discovery, make a list of all the things you are 'good at' or things you enjoy doing. Ask yourself, what are my spiritual or natural gifts? What has God already spoken to me about my gifts and calling? What talents do other people say I have? What is my passion? How can I use them to be a blessing to others and myself? It has been my experience that other people see you more gifted than you see yourself. What seems ordinary and effortless to you is the uniqueness that sets you apart. From an early age, I have been good at speaking, organization, and being a leader. These natural talents have transcended and developed even more in my calling as a pastor, to preach the gospel and being the administrator for our ministry. Identifying my spiritual gifts has helped me understand my kingdom assignment and write out the vision to carry it out.

Take the list of gifts you have written down. Pray and ask God to reveal to you any other gifts you may have. Write what comes to mind. As you write, keep these questions in mind - How do you see yourself operating in ministry? How do you see yourself using your spiritual gifts in the marketplace or your local ministry? How do my gifts impact my family, etc.?

How do you plan to go forth in what God has called you to do? Write out how you want to use each gift, and where you can make an impact on the lives of others. Whether you use our gifts and talents in ministry or the marketplace, the word of God tells us to fan the flame – use the small flicker to make the gift of God spread, use the flame to add more fire, increase the flame (the passion, the God-given desire), and spread it to others.

As you go forth, don't be afraid; don't shrink back down. Go forth! God gave you power, love, and self-control, which is everything you need as you pursue your vision and dreams. All of this is to be used to glorify God!

For this reason I remind you to fan into flame the gift of God, which is in you through the laying on of my hands. For the Spirit God gave us does not make us timid, but gives us power, love and self-discipline. (2 Tim. 1:6-7)

Stars ★ have been added beside certain Scriptures to indicate what I believe are *"Power Points of Promise"* concerning gifts, talents, and callings. My hope and prayer is for an awakening to take place in your life. Awaken and make full use of your gifting! God has given you everything you need. It's inside you. You must continue to stir it up, pull it out and make full use of it!

I want to encourage you to fill out every page of this book. Keep the writings close to your heart, remembering how very blessed and gifted you are. I admonish you to use all your gifts and talents to glorify the LORD Jesus Christ!

You are *Purged, Purified and Postured Gifts!*

Natasha Meona James
MEona Ministries Founder

★ 2 Corinthians 9:15

"Thanks be to God for His indescribable gift!"

 Habakkah 2:2

"Then the Lord answered me and said, "Record the vision And inscribe it on tablets, That [b]the one who [c]reads it may run."

_____
_____
_____
_____
_____
_____
_____
_____
_____
_____
_____

1 Peter 4:10

"As each one has received a special gift, employ it in serving one another as good stewards of the manifold grace of God."

Romans 11:29
"for the gifts and the calling of God are irrevocable."

_____
_____
_____
_____
_____
_____
_____
_____
_____
_____
_____
_____
_____
_____
_____

Romans 12:6

"Since we have gifts that differ according to the grace given to us, each of us is to exercise them accordingly: if prophecy, according to the proportion of his faith;"

_____
_____
_____
_____
_____
_____
_____
_____
_____
_____
_____
_____

Ephesians 2:8

"For by grace you have been saved through faith; and that not of yourselves, it is the gift of God;"

 2 Timothy 1:6

"For this reason I remind you to kindle afresh the gift of God which is in you through the laying on of my hands."

Ephesians 4:7

"But to each one of us grace was given according to the measure of Christ's gift."

1 Corinthians 12:7

"But to each one is given the manifestation of the Spirit for the common good."

 James 1:17

"Every good thing given and every perfect gift is from above, coming down from the Father of lights, with whom there is no variation or shifting shadow."

_____
_____
_____
_____
_____
_____
_____
_____

★ 1 Timothy 4:14

"Do not neglect the spiritual gift within you, which was bestowed on you through prophetic utterance with the laying on of hands by the presbytery."

_____
_____
_____
_____
_____
_____
_____
_____
_____
_____
_____

John 4:10

"Jesus answered and said to her, "If you knew the gift of God, and who it is who says to you, 'Give Me a drink,' you would have asked Him, and He would have given you living water."

_____
_____
_____
_____
_____
_____
_____
_____
_____
_____

 1 Peter 4:11

"Whoever speaks, is to do so as one who is speaking the utterances of God; whoever serves is to do so as one who is serving by the strength which God supplies; so that in all things God may be glorified through Jesus Christ, to whom belongs the glory and dominion forever and ever. Amen."

_____
_____
_____
_____
_____
_____
_____
_____
_____
_____

 1 Corinthians 12:28

"And God has appointed in the church, first apostles, second prophets, third teachers, then miracles, then gifts of healings, helps, administrations, various kinds of tongues."

_____
_____
_____
_____
_____
_____
_____
_____
_____

 Ephesians 3:7

"of which I was made a minister, according to the gift of God's grace which was given to me according to the working of His power."

_____
_____
_____
_____
_____
_____
_____
_____
_____
_____

 Ecclesiastes 5:19

"Furthermore, as for every man to whom God has given riches and wealth, He has also empowered him to eat from them and to receive his reward and rejoice in his labor; this is the gift of God."

_____
_____
_____
_____
_____
_____
_____
_____
_____

Psalm 127:3

"Behold, children are a gift of the LORD, The fruit of the womb is a reward."

_____
_____
_____
_____
_____
_____
_____
_____
_____
_____
_____
_____
_____
_____

 1 Corinthians 12:31

"But earnestly desire the greater gifts. And I show you a still more excellent way."

 2 Timothy 1:7

"For God has not given us a spirit of timidity, but of power and love and discipline."

_____
_____
_____
_____
_____
_____
_____
_____
_____
_____
_____
_____
_____

Matthew 25:15

"To one he gave five talents, to another, two, and to another, one, each according to his own ability; and he went on his journey."

_____

_____

_____

_____

_____

_____

_____

_____

_____

_____

_____

 Proverbs 18:16

"A man's gift makes room for him And brings him before great men."

_____
_____
_____
_____
_____
_____
_____
_____
_____
_____
_____
_____
_____

MEona
MINISTRIES

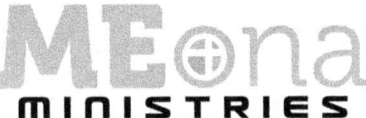

1 Corinthians 12:4

"Now there are varieties of gifts, but the same Spirit"

 1 Corinthians 12:8

"For to one is given the word of wisdom through the Spirit, and to another the word of knowledge according to the same Spirit;"

_____
_____
_____
_____
_____
_____
_____
_____
_____
_____
_____

 Exodus 31:3

"I have filled him with the Spirit of God in wisdom, in understanding, in knowledge, and in all kinds of craftsmanship",

_____
_____
_____
_____
_____
_____
_____
_____
_____
_____
_____

 Matthew 25:18

"But he who received the one talent went away, and dug a hole in the ground and hid his master's money".

 Ephesians 4:8

"Therefore it says, "WHEN HE ASCENDED ON HIGH, HE LED CAPTIVE A HOST OF CAPTIVES, AND HE GAVE GIFTS TO MEN."

_____
_____
_____
_____
_____
_____
_____
_____
_____

 1 Corinthians 12:1

"Now concerning spiritual gifts, brethren, I do not want you to be unaware"

1 Kings 10:10

She gave the king a hundred and twenty talents of gold, and a very great amount of spices and precious stones. Never again did such abundance of spices come in as that which the queen of Sheba gave King Solomon.

 Matthew 25:28

'Therefore take away the talent from him, and give it to the one who has the ten talents.

 Romans 12:4

For just as we have many members in one body and all the members do not have the same function,

 1 Corinthians 14:1

Pursue love, yet desire earnestly spiritual gifts, but especially that you may prophesy.

 1 Corinthians 12:10

and to another the effecting of miracles, and to another prophecy, and to another the distinguishing of spirits, to another various kinds of tongues, and to another the interpretation of tongues.

_____
_____
_____
_____
_____
_____
_____
_____
_____
_____

★ 1 Corinthians 14:12
So also you, since you are zealous of spiritual gifts, seek to abound for the edification of the church.

 Luke 19:17

"And he said to him, 'Well done, good slave, because you have been faithful in a very little thing, you are to be in authority over ten cities.

 1 Corinthians 1:7

so that you are not lacking in any gift, awaiting eagerly the revelation of our Lord Jesus Christ

 Matthew 25:22

"Also the one who had received the two talents came up and said, 'Master, you entrusted two talents to me. See, I have gained two more talents.

_____
_____
_____
_____
_____
_____
_____
_____
_____

★ Philippians 4:17

Not that I seek the gift itself, but I seek for the profit which increases to your account.

 Exodus 35:35

"He has filled them with skill to perform every work of an engraver and of a designer and of an embroiderer, in blue and in purple and in scarlet material, and in fine linen, and of a weaver, as performers of every work and makers of designs.

_____
_____
_____
_____
_____
_____
_____

 Matthew 25:29

"For to everyone who has, more shall be given, and he will have an abundance; but from the one who does not have, even what he does have shall be taken away

_____
_____
_____
_____
_____
_____
_____
_____
_____

 Luke 19:13

"And he called ten of his slaves, and gave them ten minas and said to them, 'Do business with this until I come back.

Prophetess Natasha James resides in Durham, NC with her husband and family. She is the founder of MEona Ministries, which is an outreach ministry providing spiritual guidance, food, and clothes to the needy. Her passion for prayer, teaching the word of God and evangelism drives her to share the gospel of Jesus Christ to all who will listen.

Despite all obstacles she keeps the flame burning for Jesus by keeping a praise on her lips! Remembering God's faithfulness, she reflects on JESUS' matchless resume! He is forever faithful and more than qualified; no matter what life brings! He's too awesome to articulate, but she expresses herself passion for him with Psalm 34:1 – I will bless the LORD at all times; His praise shall continually be in my mouth.

Gift and talent defined

gift

[gift]SHOW IPA
/ gift /PHONETIC RESPELLING
SYNONYMS|EXAMPLES|WORD ORIGIN
SEE MORE SYNONYMS FOR gift ON THESAURUS.COM

---

noun

something given voluntarily without payment in return, as to show favor toward someone, honor an occasion, or make a gesture of assistance; present.

the act of giving.

something bestowed or acquired without any particular effort by the recipient or without its being earned: Those extra points he got in the game were a total gift.

a special ability or capacity; natural endowment; talent: the gift of saying the right thing at the right time.

verb (used with object)

to present with as a gift; bestow gifts upon; endow with.

to present (someone) with a gift: just the thing to gift the newlyweds.

talent

[tal-uhnt]SHOW IPA
/ tæl nt /PHONETIC RESPELLING
SYNONYMS|EXAMPLES|WORD ORIGIN
SEE MORE SYNONYMS FOR talent ON THESAURUS.COM

---

noun

a special natural ability or aptitude: a talent for drawing.

a capacity for achievement or success; ability: young men of talent.

a talented person: The cast includes many of the theater's major talents.

a group of persons with special ability: an exhibition of watercolors by the local talent.

Movies and Television. professional actors collectively, especially star performers.

a power of mind or body considered as given to a person for use and improvement: so called from the parable in Matt. 25:14–30.(Dictionary.com)

Gift in scripture

1 Corinthians 12: 1 "Now about the spiritual gifts (the special endowments of supernatural energy), brethren, I do not want you to be misinformed." (Amplified Bible, Classic Edition, AMPC)

Supernatural gifts also known as spiritual gifts imparted by Holy Spirit to believers to help in ministry of the church.

The gift of prophesy
The gift of faith
The gift of speaking in tongues
The teaching gift
The revelation (revelator)
The gift of speaking in other tongues - ability to speak in unknown languages (speaking in tongues)
The interpretation of tongues – (interpret what is being said in unknown language)
The gift of wisdom (to give wise advice -wisdom)
The gift of knowledge
The gift of faith
The gift of healing
The gift of miracles (able to perform)
The gift of discerning of spirits (God's spirit vs another spirit speaking)
Apostles (special messengers)
Prophets (inspired preachers and expounders) Office of the Prophet
Teachers
Those who do miracles – wonder workers
Those who have the gift of healing -healers
Those who can help others – helpers

Those who can get others to work together – organizers and administrators
Those who pray in tongues

Romans 12:6-8 (AMPC)

6 Having gifts (faculties, talents, qualities) that differ according to the grace given us, let us use them: [He whose gift is] prophecy, [let him prophesy] according to the proportion of his faith;

7 [He whose gift is] practical service, let him give himself to serving; he who teaches, to his teaching;

8 He who exhorts (encourages), to his exhortation; he who contributes, let him do it in simplicity and liberality; he who gives aid and superintends, with zeal and singleness of mind; he who does acts of mercy, with genuine cheerfulness and joyful eagerness.

    Prophecy (the gift of prophesy)
    Practical service (serving gift)
    Teach
    Exhorts (speakers, orators)
    Contributes (givers)
    Gives aid and superintends (leaders)
    Does acts of mercy

1 Peter 4:10-11, (AMPC)

10 As each of you has received a gift (a particular spiritual talent, a gracious divine endowment), employ it for one another as [befits] good trustees of God's many-sided grace [faithful stewards of the [a]extremely diverse powers and gifts granted to Christians by unmerited favor].

11 Whoever speaks, [let him do it as one who utters] oracles of God; whoever renders service, [let him do it] as with the strength which God furnishes [b]abundantly, so that in all things God may be glorified through Jesus Christ (the Messiah). To Him be the glory and dominion forever and ever (through endless ages). Amen (so be it).

Ephesians 4:11-16 (AMPC)

11 And His gifts were [varied; He Himself appointed and gave men to us] some to be apostles (special messengers), some prophets (inspired preachers and expounders), some evangelists (preachers of the Gospel, traveling missionaries), some pastors (shepherds of His flock) and teachers.

12 His intention was the perfecting and the full equipping of the saints (His consecrated people), [that they should do] the work of ministering toward building up Christ's body (the church),

13 [That it might develop] until we all attain oneness in the faith and in the comprehension of the [[a]full and accurate] knowledge of the Son of God, that [we might arrive] at really mature manhood (the completeness of personality which is nothing less than the standard height of Christ's own perfection), the measure of the stature of the fullness of the Christ and the completeness found in Him.

14 So then, we may no longer be children, tossed [like ships] to and fro between chance gusts of teaching and wavering with every changing wind of doctrine, [the prey of] the cunning and cleverness of [b]unscrupulous men, [gamblers engaged] in every shifting form of trickery in inventing errors to mislead.

15 Rather, let our lives lovingly [c]express truth [in all things, speaking truly, dealing truly, living truly]. Enfolded in love, let us grow up in every way and in all things into Him Who is the Head, [even] Christ (the Messiah, the Anointed One).

16 For because of Him the whole body (the church, in all its various parts), closely joined and firmly knit together by the joints and ligaments with which it is supplied, when each part [with power adapted to its need] is working properly [in all its functions], grows to full maturity, building itself up in love.

References

https://WWW.Dictionary.com
https://WWW.Biblegateway.com

www.ingramcontent.com/pod-product-compliance
Lightning Source LLC
Chambersburg PA
CBHW081727100526
44591CB00016B/2534